First published 2008
This edition © Wooden Books Ltd 2022

Published by Wooden Books Ltd.
Glastonbury, Somerset
www.woodenbooks.com

British Library Cataloguing in Publication Data
Johnson, P.
The Little People

A CIP catalogue record for this book
may be obtained from the British Library

ISBN-10: 1-904263-99-2
ISBN-13: 978-1-904263-99-9

All rights reserved.
For permission to reproduce any part of this
enchanting little book please contact the publishers.

Designed and typeset in Glastonbury, UK.

Printed in China on FSC® certified papers by
RR Donnelley Asia Printing Solutions Ltd.

THE LITTLE PEOPLE
FAIRIES, ELVES, NIXIES, PIXIES, KNOCKERS, DRYADS & DWARVES

Paul Johnson

with occasional illustrations by Dan Goodfellow

For Freya and Danu,
May your goddesses forever watch over you.

'They could cause and cure most diseases
And knew the virtues of herbs, plants, stones,
Minerals, of all creatures, birds, beasts,
Of the four elements, stars and planets.'

THE ANATOMY OF MELANCHOLY,
ROBERT BURTON, 1621

ABOVE: *Autumn Wind*, from Australian Songs, Ida Rentoul Outhwaite, 1920.
HALF TITLE PAGE: Illustration for the *Golden Weathercock*, Alice Helena Watson, 1934.
TITLE PAGE: *What Came of Picking Flowers*, Arthur Rackham, 1916.
OVERLEAF: *The Fairies of the Serpentine*, from Peter Pan, Arthur Rackham, 1906.

CONTENTS

Introduction	1
Once Upon a Former Time	2
The Enchantment Endures	4
Wandering Between the Worlds	6
The Second Sight	8
Springs and Babbling Brooks	10
Realms of Rushing Water	12
Sand and Foam	14
Ladies of the Lake	16
Coves and Cunning Caves	18
Inside the Mountains	20
The Wild Woodland	22
The Crowd of Copses	24
Tree and Leaf	26
The Green Gallitrap	28
Vales, Valleys and Dales	30
Doors in Hollow Hills	32
Queen of the Stars	34
The Misty Meadows	36
The Muddy Marshes	38
Frolickers of Field and Farm	40
Honouring the Hearth	42
The Magic Garden	44
Journey's End	46
Glossary of Little People	48

Introduction

The enigma and identity of the little people have, through the ages of yore, vexed greater minds than thine tiny and persevered in the asking. Many lives have been touched by them, through the ancient tales that have long been told, to the fleeting glimpses that have been had of them in their natural surroundings. Our perception, like our history, has fashioned them with different cloaks of identity and appearance, made of a fabric that has been weft together with the magical glamour they have used to veil themselves from us. This glamour that they have cast over us, whose veil still enchants our vision, is perhaps the most forgotten yet finest thread of rapture they have tied to us and its knots hold fast still!

The farther back in time we tread into the green wilderness of this land the more real and part of our lives the little people become. Our forbearers, who worked with nature as the harvest of their labours, coexisted alongside the little people and accepted them as part of their daily rustic life. Legend tells that they began to disappear from our vision with the approach of the invisible century, known to us as the industrial age, and would return to it when we began to realise our folly during the ascension into the visible century.

Many have tried to classify them and yet their glamour bedazzles any attempt at clear classification as they take on the features of the environment they inhabit and display them within their characters.

With such a varied illumination of perception I present this work as more of a guideline than guide as it was by the light of such flitting luminosity that this little book of little people was written.

ONCE UPON A FORMER TIME
the threads of a lost perception

Legend tells that once, upon all lands, before any people had crossed the seas to the four corners of the earth, there existed a former race of little people much shorter than man. A long-lived and shy race, they came to know the earth's secrets well, and were so intimate with nature as to be fully a part of her, perceiving everything upon her as being alive.

Among other natural gifts, they had a vision that could pass into the subtle and spiritual otherworld of nature, and were our last ancestors who naturally accepted this vision. The beings of nature, responsible for all green verdure and growth, were visible to them, as were the passing spirits of animals and humans. They observed the earth's cosmic pulses rippling across the landscape and plotted out these veins and points of energy with the stone circles, cairns, barrows and the temples of ancient worship. Rare tales of the first tribes who traversed the seas told of these ancestral little people and their ability to pass on this secret sight to mankind. Walkers of the old paths and ancient places can sometimes reconnect to this gift and see into nature's otherworld, as they once did.

Gifted with legendary supernatural powers, the little people have continued, surviving the conversion to Christianity, although during the present time they seem less likely to appear as themselves, more often taking the form of coloured orbs or earth lights merrily moving across the landscape. But beware, the lights leads to fairyland, and following blindly can lead to tricky terrain.

ABOVE: *In this picture, Dancing Fairies, by August Malström [1829–1901] the Little People take on an ethereal quality.*
BELOW: *An Elvin Dance by Richard Doyle [1824–1883] from his In Fairyland, Pictures from the Elf-World paintings.*

THE ENCHANTMENT ENDURES
glamour, tricks and invisible flicks

In Ireland, anciently rich in fairy lore, there is an old expression known as *Foidin Seachrain* the 'stray sod', a familiar name for an age-old experience of stepping, unknowingly, onto a piece of sacred ground enchanted by the little people. This glamour sends the walker wandering, bewildered, in a completely different direction, their mind boggled as to which was their right way. Familiar marks on the land dissolve and paths or markers vanish. The seasons can change.

This mischievous sport is delighted in by most species of the little

people, who are entertained, even today, by confusing our senses and tempting the bewildered walker father and father with their beckoning luminescence (although they sometimes lead someone lost back home). Humans who have been thus led astray are known by many names; *pixie-led*, *piskie-led*, *puck-* or *pouk-ledden*. One method of dispelling this glamour was to wear one's jacket inside out.

Sometimes, when a wanderer has stepped onto enchanted ground or directly into their territory the little people may become visible to them, but only ever fleetingly between on eye blink and the next. In effect these sacred places are portals to the otherworld of nature and thus to the beings that take abode therein.

Wandering Between The Worlds
betwixt the boundaries of beauty

All natural changes in the physical terrain and spacing of the land, such as streams, rivers, knolls, woods, mountain ranges and moors function as real boundaries between the worlds of humans and the little people, and are considered to be crossover points between our world and theirs. As ancient man developed, the lay of the land gradually became partitioned into the many enclosures we have today. Divisions made by man such as thickets, hedges, fences, walls, lanes, styles and gates, separated the land and where once made in accordance and harmony with the little people. The land, at one point in her story, was sectioned out in accordance with these lays, fairy paths and habitations all being respectfully avoided. Humans were sure not to build houses, roads or any other structure over the 'fairy-paths' or ground sacred to them, for to do so would bring great misfortune and this practice still continues in Ireland today.

Crossing such divisions, whether natural or man-made can transport one directly into the fairy realm, and ancient mounds, barrows, tumuli, standing stones, circles of trees and tors are still today visited across all lands by those seeking to walk between the worlds, for such places where the realms meet are sacred ground and are avoided by ordinary folk.

Another word of warning, however. Reaching into their realms renders the wanderer under the power of the little people and only those of pure purpose can gain their respect and kindness.

TOP LEFT: Arthur Rackham, fairies in a circle, from *A Midsummer-Night's Dream*, 1908. LOWER LEFT: Arthur Rackham, *The Gnomes*, 1900. ABOVE: Mystical stones by Dan Goodfellow, 2008. BELOW: Ch. -G Petit, from *L'Ane des Korrigans* (The Fairie's Ass), Paris, 1894.

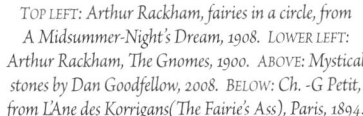

The Second Sight
the sacred science of seeing

There is much folklore concerned with seeing into the realm of fairyland, a sight that lies just beyond normal human vision. The *second sight*, as it is known in Scotland, has many facets, the main one being the constant vision into fairyland. Only a rare few individuals carry this gift, yet snatches of it can sometimes be bestowed to the true of heart. For those others wishing to perceive, stones with a naturally occurring hole in them, usually found on river-beds, can be gathered to perceive them in their otherworld. A four-leaf clover is another ancient emblem of the little people, and finding one, as well as bringing extreme good luck, can sometimes render the 'fairy vision'. Their leaves, the sole ingredient, are compounded in the magical ointment of fairy sight, which is said to render constant vision into the fairy domain after application to the eyes.

Sometimes, when the time is right, it is possible to see the little people busy in their realm. The best times to do this are during the four hinges of the day (sunrise, midday, sunset, midnight) and especially between the lights, at dawn and dusk, when day and night are equal. The chances of seeing them are also extended on the four main celebration days of the ancient pagan year (midsummer, autumn equinox, midwinter, spring equinox) and especially on the four cross-quarter which lie halfway between them.

LEFT: Elves in Woodland by Emile Daube, plate from Chez la Fée Lucine, 1930. ABOVE: Looking through a natural 'holey' stone can aid the acquisition of the Second Sight, Dan Goodfellow, 2008. BELOW: A Christmas Treat, William Heath Robinson, 1913

Springs and Babbling Brooks
pixies, nixies and silly splashes

All species of the little people simply adore water but no greater fun is had than by the *pixies* who simply worship water and love to play in it. Ancient wells and springs everywhere remain sacred to the little people, and they are the careful and wise wardens of such places. Placing offerings of money, pins, buttons, milk, cheese or objects of worth into these wells is a continuation of the belief in their magical ability to grant wishes or bestow healing and indeed all older wells are, either, wishing or healing wells.

Over time, many wells and springs have been renamed and, so, lost their connection with their true owners. Yet the tradition of tying ribbons to nearby trees to honour the little people continues today and they may still be seen dancing around many of the old wells particularly around midsummer.

The first water to be drawn from the well after the winter solstice was called the cream or flower of the waters and was especially magically powerful, being blessed by the pixies. The use of this water could improve matrimonial prospects, beauty, health and the magical ability of flying, usually granted to those who know the lore of the little people. Dew, gathered from the grass upon the four main celebration days of the year, was also exceptionally blessed by the little people, being useful for healing.

Sometimes, upon watery days, if you listen carefully, high pitched pixie laughter can be heard ringing around wells as it is replenished and refreshed.

TOP LEFT: Waterfall Nixie, Dan Goodfellow, 2008. ABOVE: The Waterfall Fairy, Ida Rentoul Outhwaite, 1921. LEFT & BELOW: A. Rackham; These Fairy Mountains, 1904; Sabrina with Water Nymphs, 1921.

REALMS OF RUSHING WATER
resident river revellers

The female *nixies* and the male *nixen* are very closely related to European *undines*, river maidens and river men. Both species of fairy are fabled and very old, yet usually appear in human form as young and beautiful, and share between them many of the same duties and powers. They are constant and highly skilled shape-shifters, but while the women tend to favour elegant fishtails the men often change into a horse, either in part or completely. The guardians of the underwater realms of the little people, they always accompany those visiting this realm. Nixies and nixen are generally inoffensive to humans. However, on occasions their mood can reflect the ever-changing waters which they inhabit, and they have been known to lure the unwary to a watery embrace.

All have a particular fondness and love of humans and tales tell of them choosing humans as their consorts. They like playing practical jokes and would often throw a human into the river once they had climbed onto the horse that they had luckily found. They have the magical power to answer any question about the present or future, the ability to play the fiddle or harp and will sometimes teach humans how to play if properly gifted.

Arthur Rackham, The Rhinemaidens and Loge, The Ring, 1910

Sand and Foam
sprites of the sea and shore

Of all of the good neighbours bound with the sea and shore none are more celebrated than the *mermaids* and *mermen*. Half human with the iridescent tail of a fish they have long flowing hair and webbed hands. Merpeople have undisputed control over the weather at sea and can calm a storm or raise a wind at will. Sailor's tales speak of the lustrous beauty of mermaids and how they occasionally choose a human as their consort, living with them either under water or on land. Mermaids carry a comb and a mirror and are sometimes seen singing whilst combing their hair on a rock out at sea. They have a great and ancient knowledge of herbs and healing and are gifted with prophecy and the granting of wishes if respectfully dealt with. They can also shape shift and often turn into seals or fish.

The Irish *Merrows* or *moruadh* are the equivalents of the English mermaids, and inhabit *Tir fo Thoinn*—the Land beneath the Waves. The most famous of them is Liban who had the tail of a salmon and swam the seas of Ireland until 558 AD; indeed some of the merpeople stayed inland after the deluge and took abode in the many inland lakes of these islands.

It is said that any mortal lucky enough to perceive the merpeople and dealing with them impeccably may have the gift of immortality bestowed upon them, or be given other treasures from the sea.

TOP LEFT: *The Little Mermaid*, Edmund Dulac, 1911. ABOVE: Frank Pape, *The Little Merman*, 1909. LEFT: *Mermaid*, Dan Goodfellow 2008. BELOW: *The Siren of Fresnaye*, Louis-Ernest Lesage [1847-1891]

LADIES OF THE LAKE
mysterious maidens of moonlight

During the light of a full moon, reflected upon a lake so still as to mirror the starlit sky an astonishingly beautiful species of the little people may sometimes be seen. The *Asrai* are gentle women of the water, many hundreds of years old, yet still very beautiful with long verdigris hair and webbed toes.

Cornish legend knows full-moon nights as *asrai nights* when these fairies come up to the water's surface to commune with the moon in all its glory. Because of their shyness the asrai are seldom seen, surfacing as little as once every century to dance under the moonlight to the music of crickets. Distant relatives of the mermaid, they cannot live on land and melt in the sun. Their Welsh cousins are the *Gwragedd Annwn* who live in sunken cities in the many lakes of Wales. Indeed every inland lake has a fairy divinity connected to it.

Like many of the fair folk these lovely creatures are known to sometimes choose mortal men as their husbands, and may choose to live the limited span of a human life or her consort may join her in their realm of lengthened fairy time, nearly becoming immortal.

Their magical masteries are formidable, yet only remote reflections remain of this knowing.

Le Spectre du Marais, Yan Dargent [1824-1899]

COVES AND CUNNING CAVES
keepers of stone, ore and metal

Beneath the earth's surface, in the warm depths of her belly, are many secret spaces and passages, more numerous and fantastic than mankind can guess at. Here is the most populated domain of the little people, for countless species take their abode in these subterranean realms.

The Cornish *Knockers*, the Welsh *Coblynau* (*goblyn*) and the Scottish *Black Dwarves* are closely related species, around a foot in height, and used to be seen dressed in the old fashioned attire of miners carrying tiny hammers, picks and lamps. Rarely seen today, but very good fortune to do so, they are benevolent to the respectful and will knock loudly where rich veins of ore and metal lie in the galleries of the mines. They know the location of all deposits of ore and metal, mineral gems and precious stones as well as hidden treasures, buried deep within the secret places of the mountains. They have been known to warn miners of cave-ins and also to cause showers of stone or rocks to fall upon the uncivil and disrespectful, particularly those who swear or whistle.

ABOVE: *Illustration from La Belle aux Clefs d'Or, Louis-Ernest Lesage [1847-1891].* BELOW: *The dwarf Mime toils over an anvil, by Arthur Rackham from The Ring, 1910.* OPPOSITE: *Cornish Knocker by Dan Goodfellow, 2008.*

CURIOUS MOUNTAIN CAVERNS
denizens of the deep beneath

The four directions of the compass, north, east, south and west, derive their names from four-famous *dwarves* (from the Old Norse *dvergr*) of Heathen tradition, *Nordri*, *Austri*, *Sudri*, and *Vestri* who, according to legend, uphold the four corners of the sky. Legendary smiths of the underworld, dwarves dwell deep within mountains, extracting ores and metals for their magical smithing work. Able to foresee the future, they can shape-shift at will and often own a magic cap, cloak, belt, or invisibility ring. Their tribal kingdoms are deep within subterranean halls inside the interiors of mountains where underground cities and palaces are fabled to be filled with treasures too precious for the sight of mortal eyes. Of all species of little people the dwarves have best continued in prosperity. Sharp and elusive, their dealings with mortals are not always friendly, yet a well-founded respect can do no wrong.

OPPOSITE: *French dwarfs, Guy Sabran, 1945.* ABOVE LEFT: *Dwarf smiths, Dan Goodfellow, 2008.*
ABOVE RIGHT: *Underworld, Emile Souvestre, 1844.* BELOW: *Princess and Trolls, John Bauer, 1913.*

The Wild Woodland
woods between the worlds

The wild woods are the last green sanctuaries of wilderness and are one of the most populated places of the little people—both sacred to and protected by them. Woods and forests are also home to the individual and collective deities governing each species of tree, plant and flower and as such are the last great entrances of initiation into the mysteries of the great earth mother herself.

Getting lost is the first step when looking for the *Heart of the Forest*. Without the help of the little people it cannot be found, but when it is, one walks through a wall of silence into a space where vision begins to looses its solidity as the web of glamour disentangles. Also found near to the Heart of the Forest are *fairy knolls* or *knowes*, small, raised mounds of earth covered in moss, grass or vegetation. Powerfully protected entrances to their realm, offerings left outside of them sometimes grant blessings in return. The fabled fairy knowe at Aberfoyle, in Scotland was where the reverend Robert Kirk entered the *Secret Commonwealth* and wrote a book bearing the same title, eventually passing from this earth into the same realm, where he remains to this day.

Rare trees consisting of several different species growing together are especially potent and venerated by the little people, both as a place of abode and as a meeting place of *Dryads*, or tree spirits. The usual offerings of milk, butter, cheese, oatmeal and bread, made at the foot or in the nook of such trees and offered without expectation, can render wondrously clear vision into their realm (for the fair folk prefer human food to their own).

ABOVE: *Tree Elf,* Dan Goodfellow 2008. RIGHT: *Dancing Fairies* by Gyo Fujikawa, 1979. BELOW: Illustration from *La Nuit Enchantée* by R. Joncour, 1945. BELOW RIGHT: *Midsummer Eve* by Edward Robert Hughes, 1908.

The Crowd of Copses
tree spirits and sprites

Trees, dryads and their resident little people all depend on each other for survival, with each species of fairy carrying the unique qualities of the tree it inhabits and is part of. If appropriately dealt with, these fair folk can bequeath great gifts of magic or healing to those who know how to ask. In times past trees were venerated as cosmic pillars, and magical flight to the upper and lower worlds was effected through working with the oldest of them.

Old *Oak Men* are the guardians of the forest, stout, strong, red-nosed little beings, who are sometimes seen tending to the growth of their young saplings whilst the *Oak Ladies* prefer to dance at the foot of their

trees. The *Elder Mother* has many little people in her branches and her wood is uniquely useful for magic—flutes made from her wood are able to call the fairies forth and a person wearing a woven headdress of her twigs and berries might be able to see them, although the wood must never be taken without first asking.

The *Ash-keys* are a gift from the *Ashmen* and used for divination, placing the leaves under one's pillow will present prophetic dreams. The white *Birch Lady* was highly honoured in years past and her wood was used for the maypoles of old, the power of her resident little people dispersing fertility across the lay of the land. The *Apple Tree Man* was the oldest tree in an orchard and the largest apples from him, known in Cornwall as the *Allen apples*, contained the blessing of abundance and prosperity when handed out during the new year.

TREE AND LEAF
hobbits and hobholes

Of all forest dwellers, none is more rarely seen than the *hobbits*. Very few accounts of them exist in written literature concerning the little people, yet they have enjoyed literary resurgence in the last several decades. They belong to the family of *hobs*, from which many descendant species exist, but who, unlike the rest of their relations, have chosen not to forge connections with mankind.

This heralds what is known in the fairy faith as the *Great Divide* and echoes the time when two branches grew separately out of the fairy folk. One stem chose to try and make mankind realise his folly as the land was urbanised, whilst the other preferred to leave him to it and take vestige wherever there was true wilderness left.

Hobbits are not ill disposed to mankind, just remote from us, choosing to take abode in the most undomesticated and secluded regions of forest. They are up to three feet high, have large feet and can be quite hairy. They are shy yet benevolent, and retain knowledge of nature's secrets that is far older than themselves. Some legends tell that they are descended from *Hobany*, the king of the little people who is in service to his Queen, *Habonde*.

OPPOSITE: *Woodland elf*, Dan Goodfellow, 2008. ABOVE LEFT: *Hat Shop Fairies*, May Gibbs, 1916. ABOVE RIGHT: *Tree Spirit* from *The Old Woman in the Wood*, Arthur Rackham, 1917. BELOW: *The Fairy Tree*, Richard Doyle, 1865.

The Green Gallitrap
a merry dance of hop, skip and trot

Upon certain days of the year, when the earth moves through the four seasons, the engaging and ancient earth-fertility dances of the little people may sometimes be beheld. So enchanting is their music, for all are extremely gifted musicians, and so alluring is their dancing that they often attract the uninvited. Those souls who join them for what seems but a short spin can leave the circle to discover that seven of our years have passed. The remains of their skipping feet leaves patches of circular bare, sacred, earth and are never entered or ploughed for fear of reprisals from the little people.

Much, if not all, of ancient paganism is rooted firmly in the realms of the little people and much lore passed from the fays to the witches, wise or cunning folk. The continuing fertility rites and dances of Morris men are ancient gambols handed down from them.

La Danse des Korrigane, Louis Dulliance, 1887.

VALES, VALLEYS AND DALES
playful pranksters of pandemonium

When Shakespeare wrote *A Midsummer's Night Dream* he may have taken his inspiration from Cwm Pwca, or Puck's Valley, a fabled magical valley in the Brecon Mountains of Wales, alive with nature spirits (in Welsh *Ellyllon*, *Dynan* or *Pwca*).

The English *Puck* or *Pouk*, the Irish *Phouka* and their cousins the Welsh *Pwca* have all enjoyed popularity since Shakespeare's time. Collectively, their favourite pastime is to mislead night travellers much in the same way as will-o-the-wisp, yet Puck is also the Mercurial trickster and

prankster and will play mischievous practical jokes on humans much to the delight of himself and his fellows.

He can shape-shift at will and turn into other species of fey as well as taking on the form of a horse, eagle, bat, or mule.

Essentially the Puka's magical powers are used to aid and help honest folk and hinder those that are ill-disposed, although he can also spread disorder wherever he pleases. This behaviour, much the same as exhibited by all fairy species, is particular to those that left for the wilderness during the Great Divide. These more untamed and little people are often less than well-respected and thus viewed more spitefully and unpleasantly than they merit.

Left: Fairies by Jo White, 1925

TOP LEFT: Puck, A Midsummer Night's Dream, Arthur Rackham, 1908. ABOVE: Fairies by John Anster Fitzgerald, 1864. BELOW LEFT: Fairy Circle, Ida Rentoul Outhwaite, 1916. BELOW: by Dan Goodfellow, 2008.

Doors in Hollow Hills
round mounds and upon the hills

The ancient mounds and barrows of Scotland, England and Wales, and also the raths of Ireland, have an intimate association with the little people. Ancient tribespeoples were sometimes buried in the soils of such places so that their souls would pass into the realm.

Upon the sacred eves of the ritual year and under the light of a full moon these ancient places are still occasionally host to the midnight fairy dance. Upon finishing, the little people quickly enter their subterranean world through a magical door, which quickly closes as the last one passes into it, mysteriously disappearing to the inquisitive. Tradition states however, that if such a place is run around nine times, and the right prayers vocalised, the door to their world may be revealed and open to the welcome.

Some of the last borders between the domesticated world and the wild untamed forces of natures were the high places of our ancient islands, their mountains, hills and mounds, and many fairy species found themselves occupying such habitations. The Irish *Tuatha dé Dannan*, the people of the goddess Danu, come to dwell in the mounds called *Sídhe*, which later became the collective name for the fair folk in Ireland. The *Bean Sídhe* were the gentle and graceful fairy-women of the mounds, later reduced in human eyes to the *banshee*, a wailing portender of life's end. Having supreme magical powers they could grant luminous blessings, healings and foretell the future of any mortal. Beautiful and intelligent, they would sometimes take captivated mortal men as their companions.

LEFT: *Entrance to the Underworld*, Dan Goodfellow, 2008. ABOVE: *The Kaatskill Mountains, Rip Van Winkle*, Arthur Rackham, 1919. BELOW: *The Gnome Kitchen*, from the Book of Gnomes, Fred E Weatherly, 1890.

QUEEN OF THE STARS
Mab, the magical matriarch

Few humans have ever gazed at the ethereal beauty of the *Fairy Queen*. Each and every species of the little people have their own particular queen yet Mab personifies them all. In later days, as with many other fay folk the Fairy Queen also had a consort, the King (*Oberon* in some sources), and in Ireland, where she goes by the name of *Medb*, all the ancient fair queens and kings are recognised as goddesses and gods.

Many true poets are gifted with the second sight, and Blake and Shelley both describe the Fairy Queen in their visionary works. Indeed, many of those that travel to the fair country as Mab's guests (and are careful enough to avoid eating the food offered there) have been notably blessed on their return with the special gifts of eloquent speech, fashionable attire and worldly success. Other fortunate humans to visit her include Thomas the Rhymer and Tam Lin, both the subject of Scottish ballads bearing their name.

OPPOSITE: *The King and Queen of Fairyland, Oberon and Titania*, Francis Danby, 1837. ABOVE: *Oberon and Titania*, Arthur Rackham, 1908. BELOW: *The Marriage of Thumbelina and the Prince*, Warwick Goble, 1913.

THE MISTY MEADOWS
echoes of leprechaun laughter

Of all the little people encountered none is more widely known then the *leprechaun* that appears in Ireland, Scotland, Wales and the North of England. Several possible Gaelic roots point to the origin of the name, referring to *lugh corpan*, 'body of light', *leith bhrogan*, the 'one-shoemaker' or *luacharma'n*, 'pygmy.'

Leprechauns are between an inch and a foot and a half tall, wear green clothes with a three-pointed hat and have old wizened, bearded, faces with red noses and twinkling eyes. They are usually heard tapping away with their tiny hammers, busy at work fixing a shoe. As the sole keepers of the knowledge of all hidden treasures they only reveal the location to whoever is lucky enough to catch and keep hold of them. Their petty cash is stored in crocks at the rainbow's end. Near hopeless to outfox, they always manifest some trick to divert their catcher's vision elsewhere and then promptly vanish, quick as a wink, laughing. Sometimes they may gift the *sparàn na scillinge, or* 'purse of the shilling', a fabulous purse which never empties of money.

The cousin of the leprechaun is the *cluirchaun*, appearing in better apparel than his cousin but, ironically, without any of their wealth. Mainly preoccupied with causing much mischief in the world of man for their own amusement, which they often do to excess, they favour food, money and particularly drink, along with stolen things. This last, when taken in their usual excess, leads to the chaos they can create overnight around the house and land.

ABOVE: *Fairies dance in a meadow beside a wood. The Haunted Park, Richard Doyle, 1875.* BELOW: *Procession and circle of fairies. The Dance of the Little People, William Holmes Sullivan [1836-1908].*

THE MUDDY MARSHES
from foolish fire to rings of power

The most frequent and widespread species of the little people, more commonly seen around the world than any other, are those that appear as iridescent and phosphorescent balls or orbs of light. Innumerable species of the little people have the ability to enter their own luminescence. They prefer to appear more often over watery earth, or buried veins of metal or ore, yet travel great distances across all terrains. In England they are *Willow-the-wisp*, in Ireland the *fairy fire* or *Teine Sidh*, in Wales *Ellylldan* and in Scotland the *Merry Dancers*.

Their favourite pastime is to mislead nighttime travellers over long distances across brake and brier. They will alluringly beckon with their luminescence and are very receptive to our interest. Humans with hard heads and hearts are often lead into ditches and bogs whilst those of lighter note are often lead to behold the symmetrically beautiful circle dances that many of these lights join at their journeys' end. Whilst following them they will usually travel off if one's awareness is diverted and travel closer and slower if they are given attention. Depending upon the individual, these lights can also lead to fairyland, or sometimes to buried treasure. Groups of five are lucky.

OPPOSITE: Will-o-the-Wisps flicker over marshland, Dan Goodfellow, 2008. ABOVE: Fairy above a muddy marsh, Iris, John Atkinson Grimshaw, 1886. BELOW: A moonlight scene, The Fairies, Gustave Dore [1832-1883].

FROLICKERS OF FIELD AND FARM
toil and soil

No species of the little people is more connected to man than the agricultural *brownies*. Belonging to a rural age now long gone they would help around the farm, sowing, ploughing, reaping and grinding the grain and other jobs. Up to three feet in size, shaggy, hairy and with very strong with old wizened faces, at one time every farm would have its own resident brownie that would help the needful and hinder the nasty and lazy, often undoing the work of many. If a gift of clothing is offered or laid to a brownie they will disappear, never to return, preferring instead a daily offering of cream, oatcakes and honey in their favourite nook either in or outside of the house. The most famous brownie appears in the ancient ballad handed down in the nursery rhyme of *Aiken Drum*.

OPPOSITE: Korrigans (little people from Brittany, France), C. Homualk, 1930. ABOVE: French goblin, Henri Riviere, 1886. BELOW: Farm Brownie, Dan Goodfellow, 2008. RIGHT: Korrigans in a French town square, Almery Lobel-Riche, 1905.

HONOURING THE HEARTH
placating the patrons of prosperity

The hearth or the fireplace was once the dwelling place of the *household spirits*, *fire sprites* and the ancestors who, in pre-classical times, were buried under it. It was the literal illumination into the otherworld. This was the favourite dwelling place of the *hobs*, *lobs*, *hobgoblins* and the *household brownie*.

Keeping the hearth clean was the first rule in attracting the little people back into the home. The would often do many domestic jobs around the household and countless tales tell of the help, gifts and good fortune the little people would give to the daily chores of man if looked after and tales of this practice even continued into the last three decades of the last century. Offerings of fresh water, milk and bread are left, nightly, by the hearth to placate the patrons of the household and even today with central heating and gas fires its quite amazing to see the results this practice can manifest around unused old hearths and blocked of chimney stacks. Horseshoes can be hung over the mantle as a welcome resting place for them. They can not abide untidiness or disrespect and will undo hard work during the night or sometimes pinch lazy humans repeatedly or make the food and furniture dance around the kitchen or house.

Undomesticated *hobthrushes* are the hobgoblins' wilder cousins and prefer the wilder places of nature. More mischievous than hobs, they can cause mayhem to those they know deserve it. Offerings left on the doorstep for them as well as for other species can sometimes ensue their blessing upon the family and house.

OPPOSITE: *Household Brownies, Dan Goodfellow, 2008.* LEFT: *The Elves and the Shoemaker, George Cruikshank [1792-1878].* BELOW: *An Old Lady and a hobthrush, Eugene Courboin, 1880.*

THE MAGIC GARDEN
plant and flower

The bottom of the garden with its boundary between the green wilderness and known world is a place where wonder always exists for children. As fairies love innocence (or inner-sense) and are gallant and proud protectors of it is no wander that they reveal themselves to their little human counterparts so much.

The little people of the flowers, herbs and plants are responsible for the growth, colour and protection of their respective plants, herbs or flowers much like the little people of the trees. Devas, or *plant spirits* and *flower fairies*, are tiny, subtle, creatures dressed in the garb and colour of their particular plant and fly, as witches do, on ragwort stems although sometimes they have iridescent wings.

The connection between the flower fairies and humans is one of the few remaining chains left unbroken for it flourishes still in our gardens. Daisy chains can be made to offer the floral fays.

Say this: *" Fairy laughter and fairy light, come and be my chosen sprite."*

OPPOSITE: *Fairy Queen and Butterflies*, Richard Doyle, 1870. ABOVE LEFT: *A Fairy Song*, Arthur Rackham, 1908. ABOVE RIGHT: *Flower Fairies*, Harold Gaze, 1929. BELOW: *Under the Dock Leaves*, Richard Doyle, 1878.

Fare Thee Well
into another world

For those that seek a glimpse of the fair folk, clover is a good place to start. The different number of leaves represent different levels of awareness and initiation in the realm of the little people and their mysteries. They are best searched for in the becoming light of dawn or the receding light of dusk. The four-leaf renders the vision whilst the five represents the knowing and understanding of their existence and the six-leaf represents initiation into their mysteries.

But a word of warning: the awakenings which can be given to the seeker may not be entirely compatible with the modern world. If you find yourself preferring to sleep on a bed of moss under the stars beneath an old oak tree rather than choosing the comfort of your bed at home, or you become suddenly uncomfortable with the thought of pruning of a tree where previously no such concerns had troubled your conscience, or you begin craving fresh spring water straight from an old well, or you find you cannot stop dancing in circles and reciting poetry whilst time and the world passes you by, well then, you'll be off with the fairies then won't you. So good luck, and until next time …

Daughter of the Sea, from The Three Golden Apples, *Arthur Rackham, 1922.*

GLOSSARY OF LITTLE PEOPLE

ANTHROPOPHAGI (ENGLAND). From the Greek meaning 'man-eating'. According to English folklore, these human-eating creatures have no head, a small brain in their groin, eyes on their shoulders and a mouth in their chests.

ASHRAYS (SCOTLAND). Ancient and pale, yet youthful-looking and dwell under the water. They are nocturnal and will melt into a rainbow pool of water if touched by the light of the sun.

ANKOU (CORNWALL, WALES, IRELAND). Face hidden by his black robes, he collects the souls of the recently deceased and escorts them to the land of the dead in his black horse-drawn cart. Also known as *Grim Reaper*, *Death*, *Father Time*.

BALLYBOGS (IRELAND). The solitary, muddy-looking guardians of the peat bogs. Short and rotund with long spindly arms and legs. May be helpful or mischievous, can only grunt, not very bright. Also *Peat Faeries*, *Mudbogs* and *Bog-a-boos* or *Boggies*.

BANSHEE (IRELAND). See *Beansidhe*.

BEAN-FIONN (IRELAND). The *White Woman* who lives in lakes, streams and rivers. Likes to drag children into and under the water and drown them. Known in England as *Jenny Greentooth*.

BEAN-SIDHE (IRELAND). Means *Woman of the Faery Mounds*, or *Woman of Peace*. Pronounced '*Banshee*'. Scottish, *Cointeach;* Cornish, *Cyhiraeth;* and Welsh, *Cyhiraeth* or *Gwrach y Rhibyn*. Full-sized female human form, dressed in white (also grey or green, red or black) with long stringy hair partially covered with hood. Some have long, fair hair which they brush with a silver comb, others a ghost-like appearance. Famous for their '*keening*' or loud, terrifying wailing, heard at night, as an omen of impending death.

BEAN-NIGE (SCOTLAND). Means *Washerwoman*. Like the Welsh *Cyhiraeth* who washes her hand at a crossroads or stream. Scottish counterpart of Irish *Banshee*.

BEAN-TIGHE (IRELAND). A faery housekeeper, a small kind elderly peasant woman, who inhabits your hearthside (especially families with Milesian ancestors), like *Brownies* of Scotland, they love to live in a friendly human house and cook after children and pets, and to finish household chores left by tired busy mothers, especially those who leave out her favourite food - fresh strawberries and cream.

BLACK ANGUS (ENGLAND and SCOTLAND). *CuSith* 'faery dog' or *Barguest*. Wales *Cwn Annwn*, where they are seen crossing moors and wastelands at night. Large black dog, bright yellow eyes, sharp fangs, wet paws, roams the countryside of the north of England, and Scotland, appearing at night to those who will die within a fortnight. Scottish Lowlanders claim he has horns.

BLUE HAG See *Cailleac Bhuer*. *Bocan* (ISLE OF SKYE). Since Medieval times, these evil creatures have existed only to attack, murder and mutilate travellers at night.

BOGGARTS (SCOTLAND). A small, squat male faery who, unlike the helpful house *Brownie*, will move in to your house take the greatest delight and pleasure in causing havoc, mayhem and destruction, usually while you sleep. Loves to torment children, stealing their food and trying to smother them at night. Known as *Padfoot* or *Hobgoblin* in Northern England, he also enjoys frightening travellers and is poisonous to touch. Also known as *Goblin*, *Boogey Man*, *Boogies*, *Boggans*, *Hobbers*, *Gobs*, *Blobs*.

BOOBRIE (SCOTLAND). Black water-bound bird, about a foot high, with large sharp claws, flies over or swims through water, in search of ships carrying sheep and cattle, which it drags into the water and eats. Will use its 3-foot bill to catch fish if desperate.

BROWNIE (SCOTLAND). *Little Man* or *House Brownie*. If he decides you are a worthy human one of these kind hearted helpful little pointy-eared men with dark eyes, long fingers, wearing a felt cap and a brown, blue or green suit, will move into a cosy part of your house (if it is warm and free of cats), and in return for milk, honey, ale and cake, will keep away evil spirits and bring you food and firewood, and might even make you the odd pair of shoes. Nocturnal and intelligent, except for the Scottish *Dobie*, who, though well-meaning, is a little clumsy. English *Hobs*, Danish *Dis*, Russian *Domonvoi*, North African *Yumboes*, Chinese *Choa Phum Phi*.

BROWN MEN (CORNWALL). Related to Scots *Brownies*, Brown men are skinny, long-armed red-haired little male faeries, devoted to protecting and healing the wildlife of Bodmin Moor. They dress in brown, well camouflaged, probably to avoid being seen by humans.

BUGGARS Dangerous shape-shifting goblins, they dwell in the astral world.

BUTTERY SPRITES (ENGLAND). *Buttery Spirits*, because of their penchant for stealing butter. Under cover of darkness, never seen by humans, they seek vengeance upon hypocrites and cheats, particularly men of the cloth.

BWAGANOD (WALES). Pronounced *boo-kah-nohd*. Welsh *goblins*,

48

who can shape-shift into any animal or human form, but only briefly, at dusk. They are not dangerous or harmful, they just seem to enjoy teasing or frightening us poor humans.

BWBACHS (WALES). Pronounced *boo-boks*. Small, fat, solitary male house faery. Wears a red hat, loincloth and cloak of animal fur. Mischievous, but basically well-meaning creature. Treat him with respect and feed him well and he might just protect your house from unwanted visitors, but he may also drive your friends and family away too! Also known as *Bookers, Bottagers*.

BWCIOD (WALES). Pronounced *bu-keyd*. Small, skinny, purple eyes, long pointy nose and fingers with massive feet, yet he moves quickly and is rarely seen by humans. Loves fire and seeks out a warm cosy human homes to inhabit. Can be a nuisance, and a nightmare to get rid of.

CAILLEAC BHUER (SCOTLAND). Pronounced *Call-y'ac v'fhoor*. Also known as the *Blue Hag, Black Annis, Stone Woman*. Dressed in black or blue tattered garments, this old woman has jagged teeth, and one large blue eye and walks the winter forest at night. Her staff is topped with a crow's head and she buries it under a tree in summer. If you can find it, you will have power over all human destiny.

CHURN MILK PEG and MELCH DICK (ENGLAND). Peg is female, Dick is male. Small dwarf faeries who wear peasant clothes, their job is to protect nut and fruit bushes and trees, by giving unpleasant symptoms to those who dare steal from them. Also known as *Acorn Lady* and *Melsh Dick*.

CLURICHAUN (Ireland). Pronounced *Kloo-ree-kahn*. A close relative of the *leprechaun*, this solitary male faery wears a red hat, is usually cheery and intoxicated. In return for a constant supply of booze, he will guard your wine cellar from thieves and prevent any mishaps. Treat him well, or he'll trash the place.

CORRIGANS *Korrigans* (CORNWALL). Descended from the nine holy druidesses of ancient Gaul, they are female guardians of springs and fountains found near standing stones. Every Spring, they drink the secrets of poetry and wisdom from a crystal goblet.

CU SITH – see *Black Angus*.

DEVA (ISLE OF MAN, ENGLAND). Originally from Persia. Meaning 'Shining One', a deva appears as a bright light. They are golden faeries, or nature spirits clothed in colourful robes. They are shy, nature loving beings, inhabiting trees and lakes.

DINNSHENCHAS (IRELAND). Shape-shifting dwarf faeries, in service to Irish Faery/Goddess Aine, protecting cattle and avenging women who have been raped or harmed by men.

DOBIE (ENGLAND). In the North of England a Dobie is a kind-hearted, helpful but stupid *Brownie*, or house-faery. The Dobie of West Yorkshire, however, is a purely evil faery, who hangs around in old farmhouses and outbuildings, near old towers and bridges, waiting to jump out and garrotte passing horsemen.

DRAKE (ENGLAND). Also *Germany* & *Scandanavia*. Extremely

The Enchantment, H. J. Ford, 1897.

benevolent house faeries, dressed in little red caps and suits. They will keep your firewood dry and bring you gifts of gold and grain, in return for food, respect and the warmth of your fireside. Rarely seen, but are more commonly noticeable by their revolting sulphurous stench. When flying, they appear as a fireball with a flaming tail. Their spirits were once kept imprisoned in carved mandrake roots.

DRYADS (CELTIC COUNTRIES). Tree-dwelling *nymphs*, especially '*faery willows*', which have been known to uproot and walk around at night. Usually seen as a wisp of coloured light around a tree. They love to dance and sing beautiful songs. Not dangerous but unlucky to see or make friends with them. Taught the Druids the secrets of tree magic, divination and astral travel. Gaelic name is '*Sidhe Draoi*, or '*Faery Druids*'.

DUERGARRS (ENGLAND). Pronounced *doo-ay-gahrs*. Malicious little prankster faeries, who wear lambskin jackets, moleskin shoes and green hats. They love to play tricks and confuse travellers who dare to venture too close to the faery paths, which they guard.

DUNTERS (ENGLAND, SCOTLAND). Border faeries, or '*Powries*', who haunt the old peel towers. They are said to be the spirits of the sacrificial victims, whose blood was sprinkled on the foundations. They make strange noises, an omen of death or misfortune, usually the sound of flax being beaten or barley being ground, or sometimes they just moan and wail loudly.

DWEORG (ENGLAND). Old English demon or dwarf. Anglo Saxons would use *dweorge duostle* or *pennyroyal* for the relief of headaches inflicted on them by dwarves.

EACHRAIS URLAIR (SCOTLAND). Mischievous Scottish female faery, uses her magic wand to transform people into animals, and loves to incite mischief in others, especially children.

EARTH FAERY Faeries or *nature spirits* who live under the earth in caves or faery mounds.

ELDER MOTHER (ENGLAND). Guardian of the English elder tree. One must seek her permission before picking berries. She will inflict disease on the livestock of anyone who dares fell an elder.

ELEMENTALS Ancient science and alchemists believed mortal creatures consisted of varying mixtures of these four elements, but the elementals were pure forms of only one: *Gnomes* – Earth, *Sylphs* – Air, *Salamanders* – Fire, *Nereids* – Water. Some occultists believe that faeries are elementals. Often used as a general word for nature faeries.

ELF FIRE or ELF LIGHT (ENGLAND). Another name for *Will O' The Wisp*.

ELFAME Scottish name for Faeryland.

ELLYLLONS (CORNWALL, WALES). Tiny elf-like creatures, who dwell in hollows, dingles and inland lakes, particularly Dosmary Pool in Cornwall. They ride eggshells and wear mittens made from foxglove flowers. They eat fairy butter and fairy food such as toadstools. They guard the domain of the Lady of the Lake, of Arthurian legend.

ELVES Elves exist in many countries, but the English ones are small, plump and usually friendly faeryfolk, who usually live underground, in troops ruled by a king or queen. They dress in green or white. The name sometimes refers to small boy faeries, or mischievous tree spirits. In Scotland they are larger, human size creatures, who came from the land of *Elfame*, often kidnapping humans and killing cattle.

FACHAN (SCOTLAND). The faery of *Glen Etive*, Argyll. Odd-looking solitary fellow with only one of each eye, hand, arm, leg, foot, toe, which are all located in a row down the centre of his hairy and feathered body. Hates all living creatures, and is particularly jealous of birds, because he longs to be able to fly. He attacks humans with his spiked club, should they venture near his mountain home.

FAEU BOULANGER (GUERNSEY). Another version of *Will O' The Wisp*, seen as a ball of fire and said to be a cursed spirit, guarding hidden treasure. If you see it rolling towards you, you must turn your clothes inside out, and it will vanish.

FAIRY English word, from the French word '*fée*', and the Latin '*fatare*', meaning 'to enchant'. Originally called '*fays*' in English, the word 'faerie' was later used to refer to the little folk. It was once considered bad luck to name them at all, as it might offend them. Better to say '*little people*' and other less specific terms. Also *Fayerye*, *fairje*, *fayre*, *faery*.

FARISEES Fairies, from Somerset and Suffolk.

FEAR SIDHE Generic term for male faeries in Irish Gaelic. Also *Fir Sidhe, Far Shee*.

FEAR SIDHEAN (Scotland). Highland word for fairy men.

FEATHAG (ISLE OF MAN). Manx faeries, who live in elder trees, gathering to mourn whenever one is felled.

FEEORIN Small green-skinned faeries from Lancashire. Wear red caps, are usually helpful, love music and dancing.

FERIERS (SUFFOLK). Another word for faeries.

FERISH *Ferrish Ferrishyn Fireesin* (ISLE OF MAN). Usually house faeries who sometimes help with the harvest. Some say they steal human babies, leaving a *changeling* in their place.

FERISHERS Word for faeries from Suffolk.

FERLIES Another word for faeries in the north of England.

FETCH (ENGLAND, SCOTLAND). Faery double. If you meet your fetch, it is an omen of death. Similar to the German '*Doppelganger*'.

FIERY DRAKE (ENGLAND). From the Peak District. A ball of flames that guides miners to the richest seams of ore.

FIN FOLK (SCOTLAND, CORNWALL, WALES). Anthropomorphic faeries, not harmful, but usually avoid humans, although legend has it that a chosen few have been taken down beneath the lochs of Scotland to their kingdom, '*Finfolkaheem*', a utopian paradise encased in glass, where they tend gardens full of beautiful, brightly coloured flowers and lush greenery. Also *Sea Gardeners, Lady's Own*.

FIR BOLG (IRELAND). The people of the bogs, who ruled Ireland until defeated by the *Tuatha Dé Danaan*, then became Ireland's first race of faeries. Sometimes described as giants, but usually three feet tall and dressed in red. They live in old earthworks, or *raths*, and hate iron and Christian symbols, especially holy water.

FIR DARRIG *Feardurg Firdhearga* (IRELAND, SCOTLAND). Dangerous, ugly, fat, hairy, scruffily dressed, usually in red, with dark skin, long snout and a rat-like tail. Carries a '*shillelagh*', a skull-topped walking stick. Good swimmers, they live near the sea, swamps or marshes, where they find rotten sea carrion to eat. Forgetful people, another word for faeries, Scotland.

FORMORIANS *Formors* (IRELAND). Strangely deformed sea creatures with one eye in the centre of their forehead, three rows of sharp teeth, one leg and one hand. Descendents of a faery race banished to the sea by the *Tuatha Dé Danaan*, they can only come ashore at night.

FOX FIRE and FRIAR'S LANTERN (ENGLAND). Alternative

50

names for *Will o' the Wisp*.

FRAIRIES (ENGLAND). Another name for faeries.

FRIDEAN (SCOTLAND). Faeries who live under rocks and are the guardians of the roads of Scotland. If you leave them out offerings of bread and milk, they will ensure you have a safe journey.

FUATH (IRELAND, SCOTLAND). Pronounced *foo-ah*. Water faeries, usually evil. Human-like, green clothes, body covered in yellow fur, or sometimes just a yellow mane. Fuath have webbed toes, a tail, large eyes but no nose. They sometimes marry humans. They dislike sunlight and cold steel is deadly to them.

GANCANAGH (IRELAND). Known in Scotland and Cornwall as the *Gancaner*. Rarely seen solitary male faery or *elf*, who waits in lonely places to seduce mortal women, who then pine for him and die of a broken heart. He has black eyes and appears to smoke an Irish clay pipe, but does not inhale, because faeries don't like smoke.

GEANCANACH (IRELAND, HEBRIDES). Tiny pixie-like *sprites* or house faeries with large slanting eyes and pointy ears. They have wings but cannot fly, although they love to disappear then appear instantly somewhere else. They are mischievous pranksters but they will guard your hearth in return for a cosy warm fire and some milk.

GHILLIE DHU *Ghille Dubh* (SCOTLAND). A solitary tree spirit, protecting them from humans. He has black hair and is camouflaged with green leaves and moss, so he can hide and reach out and grab a passing human and enslave them forever. Sometimes returns children who have been lost in the forest, safely back to their homes.

GIRLE GUARLE (IRELAND). Irish faery, similar to *Rumpelstiltskin* and *Tom Tit Tot*. She agreed to spin flax for a busy mortal woman, as long as she remembered her name. But she bewitched the woman and she forgot. The woman happened upon a ring of faeries, singing about *Girle Guarle*. When she told the faery she remembered her name, she was so angry she disappeared in a terrible rage, leaving behind all the spun flax.

GLASHTIN *Glastyn* (ISLE OF MAN, OUTER HEBRIDES). Various descriptions have been reported. Some say they are water horses, with their hooves back to front, others that they are half-horse and half-bull or cow. They are shape-shifting *goblins*, who appear in human form as very handsome men, hypnotising and luring young women to the sea, where they devour them.

GLAISTIG (SCOTLAND). Small Scottish female faery, dressed in green, long yellow hair, at a distance young and beautiful, but close up her face is pale and grey. She mourns death or illness with a *Banshee*-like wail.

GLASHAN *Glaisein* (ISLE OF MAN). Strong naked Manx house faeries, particularly helpful to farmers. Have been known to magnetise stones to pull cars off the road. Can shapeshift into young foals or lambs. The males sometimes rape mortal women.

GNOMES Originally earth spirits, or *elementals*, gnome means 'earth-dweller'. Guardians of the earth, more recently very popular with gardeners who depict them as white-haired little men dressed in red. Able to move through the earth, as birds through the air, and live for a thousand years.

GOBLIN Unpleasant, ugly, mischievous, deformed little human-like creatures. Usually live in groups underground, in churchyards, amongst ancient tree roots, or sometimes move in with humans. Evil pranksters who cause harm to humans for their amusement. Sometimes depicted wearing leather armour and carrying spears.

GOOD NEIGHBOURS *Good People* (SCOTLAND, ENGLAND, IRELAND). Faery folk.

GOOSEBERRY WYFE (ISLE OF WIGHT). Guardian of the gooseberries, in the form of a big fat hairy caterpillar.

GRUAGACH (SCOTLAND, IRELAND). In Scotland they are a long-haired and hairy form of *Glaistig*. Male or female, they live in stately homes and castles, and busy themselves at night with domestic chores or rearranging furniture. When angry they play pranks and make a mess, but in return for milk they will protect your cattle. In Ireland the name is used for ogres, goblins, giants, magicians and druids.

GREEN LADIES Tree faeries who dwell in oak, elm, yew, apple, willow and holly. May seek terrible revenge if you cut down one of

Wood Elves Hiding, Richard Doyle, 1890.

51

their trees, but will bless you and reward you with prosperity if you plant primroses at their feet. In Scotland and Wales this is a generic term used for green faeries and sometimes ghosts. Also *Dryads*.

GREEN MAN Green nature spirit, depicted as a head with leaves and branches coming from its mouth. Powerful faeries who fire deadly *elf* bolts or flint arrows when offended by crimes against nature. Also known as *Hob, Hodekin, Robin, Robin Goodfellow* or *Robin Hood*.

GREENCOATIES (LINCOLNSHIRE). Faery folk, particularly those who are green or dressed in green. Also *Greenies* (Lancashire).

GREMLINS Modern English faeries, apparently first discovered by Air Force Pilots in WWII. Said to be about 6-20 inches high, green, blue or grey, with big ears or horns.

GRIGS (BRITAIN). Tiny, jolly little faeries, dressed in green with red caps made of flowers. In Somerset, the smallest apples left on the trees for the faeries are known as '*griggling apples*'.

GRIM (ENGLAND). Hooded English *goblin*, his appearance frightening the simple and his terrible screeching at the windows of a sick man scaring him to death.

GRYPHONS (WALES). Welsh faeries with head of a horse and body of a goat, who can speak any human language and destroy crops if not harvested before Halloween.

GUILLYN VEGGEY (ISLE OF MAN). Manx word for faery, meaning '*little boy*'.

HEATHER PIXIES (SCOTLAND, YORKSHIRE). Live amongst heather, especially on the moors, avoiding human contact. Little pranksters with golden auras and translucent wings, who spend their time spinning flax.

HENKIES (SHETLAND, ORKNEY). Another name for the *Trows*. Small, grotesque little beings, who walked and danced with a limp or '*henk*' and clasped their hands around their knees.

HINKY-PUNK (SOMERSET/DEVON). Another version of *Will 'O The Wisp*, found around the Somerset/Devon border. Reported to have one leg and a light and lead you into bogs. Similar to the *Hunky Punky* found in Cornwall.

HOBGOBLINS (ENGLAND, SCOTLAND). Common English house faeries, or *hearth spirits*, love to be warm and cosy next to the fire or hob. One or two feet high, with dark skin, either naked or wearing brown tattered clothes. Usually friendly helpful and domesticated, particularly enjoy farm work. Like to steal from misers, and are said to guard treasure. Don't upset them, or they turn into very unpleasant *Boggarts*. Scottish Hobgoblins are shapeshifters, often called *Brags*. Also *Hob-gob, Tom-Tit, Robin Round Cap, Hob-Thrush, Goblin-Groom, Billeboinkers, Blobins, Gooseys, Hobmen* or *Hobs*.

HOBYAHS (ENGLAND, SCOTLAND). Evil goblins who kidnap and enslave humans, taking them down mines to dig for gold, and then eating them. Apparently they are no more, having all been eaten by a Black Dog.

HODEKIN (ENGLAND). Forest *elf*. Also, another name for *Robin Hood*.

HODGEPOCHER *Hodgpoker* (ENGLAND). English house faery or *Hobgoblin*.

HOGBOY *Hogboon Hug-Boy* (ORKNEY). Shadowy fellows, live in the mounds of Orkney. They protect pets and farm animals from the *Trows* and mend farming equipment, in return for offerings of ale and milk. If anyone dare destroy or disturb a mound, a *hogbot* will appear as a little grey man and attack them.

HOOKIES (ENGLAND). Lincolnshire term for *Faeries*.

HOUSE FAERY / HOME SPRITE A faery or spirit which looks after your home, performing domestic chores while you sleep, in return for food, drink and a warm place to sleep by the hearth. Some are pranksters, especially when offended, and will break or hide things and generally make a mess.

HYTERS OR HYTER SPRITES (LINCOLNSHIRE, EAST ANGLIA). Small, shapeshifting green eyed faeries, often appear as birds, particularly sand-martins, buzzards or vultures. Not keen on humans, but protective of human children, sometimes returning those who get lost. They will often gather in groups and buzz or mob people, especially neglectful parents, apparently only to frighten, not to harm.

IRISH ELVES Generic term for wingless faeries. Male, female and child dwarves dressed in blue or green with red caps. Live in troops under the ground, among the tree roots of sacred trees. Come out at night to help sick animals. Usually avoid humans, but will occasionally reward one who shows particularly selfless behaviour. *Little People, Wee Folk, Little Fellers*.

IMP Wicked faery or small demon. From the Old English '*impe*', meaning '*young shoot*', possibly implying that an imp is an off-shoot of the devil. Malicious little black creatures. They can be charmed, particularly through their love of music, to do good deeds, but even then, they can't be trusted completely. Also the name for a witch's *familiar* in the Middle Ages. *Ympe. Impet* (small Imp).

IRISH SEA WATER GUARDIANS (ISLE OF MAN). Water guardian faeries, or *sea sprites*. Both male and female, beautiful, tiny, only a few inches high, with a greeny-blue aura. Sail on broken eggshells, or surf on seashells, guarding the Irish Sea and all living creatures within it. Serve *Manaan*, the Sea God. Also known as *Undines*.

JACK FROST (ENGLAND). English faery, depicted in white, with sharp pointy features, covered in icicles. He brings the frost, leaving the beautiful ice crystal patterns on your window panes on a cold morning.

JACK-A-LANTERN (ENGLAND). English bog or marsh faery, haunting the marshes at night, bewitching travellers with his glowing flames, luring them to their deaths. Today the name given to Hallowe'en pumpkin lanterns. Also *Jack O'Lantern, Jacky Lantern*.

Gustave Doré, from The Idylls of the King, 1878.

KELPIES (SCOTLAND). Small, round, shapeshifting *water faeries*. Usually appear as grey horses, luring humans to mount and ride them, only to run into the water and drown their passengers, then devour them. Similar to the Irish *Uisges*, the Cornish *Shoney* and the Welsh *Ceffyl Dwr*, as well as the *Nuggies* of Shetland and Orkney.

KILMOULIS (SCOTLAND). Grotesque faery or *Brownie*, no mouth, eats by stuffing food into huge nose. In return for a warm place to sleep by the oven (*killogee*), he serves and protects the miller and his family, wailing to warn them of impending illness or misfortune, and fetching the midwife when necessary. Enjoys playing pranks, such as blowing ashes over shelled oats.

KNOCKERS (DEVON, CORNWALL). Friendly *mine spirits*, said to be the ghosts of the Jews who worked there long ago. Small, ugly, skinny, hooked noses, thin wide mouths, they dress in miners' clothes with leather aprons, carrying tiny picks. Abide in mines and caves, and in return for a nice pasty will make knocking sounds to direct miners to rich veins of tin, or to warn of danger, or to lead them to a buried miner after a cave-in. *Buccas, Gathorns, Nickers, Nuggies, Spriggans*. Similar to the Welsh *Coblynaus*, and the Scottish *Black Dwarves*.

KNOCKY-BOH (ENGLAND). *Boggart*, or *poltergeist*, makes a '*poltering*' (knocking or rattling) sound from behind the walls or wood panelling of houses, especially at night, waking the family and frightening children.

KNOPS (WEST MIDLANDS). Terrifying demon horses, possibly the source of the '*All Souls Day*' (November 22nd) custom, of covering a model of a horse's head in a sheet to frighten people.

KOW Old Northern English word for faery or spirit.

LADY OF THE LAKE Sometimes known as *Vivienne*, or *Nimue*, or *Niniane*. In Arthurian legends she is a beautiful water faery who steals Lancelot from his mother, taking him to her underwater kingdom, where she nurtures him into a great man. She gives him his magical sword *Excalibur*, then upon his death, takes them both back to the Isle of Avalon.

LEANAN SIDHE *Leanhaun Shee* (IRELAND) *Leannan Sith* (SCOTLAND) *Lhiannan Shee* (ISLE OF MAN). Seductively beautiful *fairy mistress* or *vampire faery*, usually female. Visible only to her lover, in whom she inspires great poetry and music, giving him strength in battle and a successful career. Also said to reduce his earthly life span.

LEPRECHAUN (IRELAND). Small, male dwarf faery, dressed in green, with silver-buttoned waistcoats, leather aprons, blue stockings and silver-buckled shoes. They wear cocked or tri-cornered hats which they can turn upside down and spin upon. Love whiskey, tobacco, music, dancing, fox-hunting and riddles. Also *Leprechan, Leprochaune, Luchorpan, Lubrican, Lubberkein, Luricane, Lurican, Lurikeen, Lurigadaune, Leprehaun, Lepracaun, Leipreachan*.

LESIDHE (IRELAND). Pronounced *Lay-shee*. Forest guardian, usually solitary, mostly nocturnal, disguised as foliage, only visible when moving. Imitates mocking birds, or human sounds to confuse and lead human travellers astray, to avenge their mistreatment of nature.

LITTLE DARLINGS   Euphemism for faeries. Also *Little Folk*, *Little People*.

LOB (WALES, ENGLAND). House faery, attracted to unpleasant emotions and arguments. Sometimes described as a small dark blob, intent on making trouble, delighting in human misery but usually too lazy to bother. Also *Lob-Lie-By-The-Fire*, *Lubbard Fiend* or *Lubbar Fend*.

LOIREAG (HEBRIDES). Small, stubborn, cunning female water faery, dressed in white. Patroness of spinning. Punishes those who neglected the traditions and ceremonies associated with warping, weaving and washing the web. A lover of music, she is easily offended by less than perfect singing by the weavers.

LUNANTISHEE *Lunantisidhe* (IRELAND). *Moon faeries*, guardians of the blackthorn bushes. Bald old men with pointy ears and long teeth, arms and fingers. They love to dance under the light of the moon, and punish anyone who dares to cut their bushes on *Samhain* (original *All Hallows Day*, 11th November) or *Beltane* (original *May Day* 11th May).

LY ERG (SCOTLAND). Small faery, who dresses as a soldier. If he should stop and raise his bloodstained right hand to challenge you, run away, for if you fight him you will die within a fortnight.

MAB (WALES, ENGLAND). Best known as *Queen* or *muse* of the *Welsh Faeries*, the *Ellyllon*. Described by Shakespeare in Romeo and Juliet as '*midwife*' of their magic and dreams.

MAIGHDEAN MARA *Maighdean Na Tuinne* (SCOTLAND). Mermaids.

MAL-DE-MER (CORNWALL, BRITTANY). French meaning '*Evil of the Sea*' or '*sea sickness*'. They shine bright lights to lure ships onto rocks at night, fooling sailors into thinking they are safely in the harbour. They then possess the souls of the dead sailors.

MANANNAN (ISLE OF MAN). Chief of the Manx faeries. Irish sea God with invincible sword and armour. Protector of the island to which he gave its name. When the *Tuatha Dé Danaan* fled defeated, he gave them the power to shapeshift into a herd of magical pigs that, when eaten, came back to life the next day.

MERMAIDS *Mermen Merpeople* (SCOTLAND, ENGLAND, IRELAND). Head and body of a human, fish from the waist down. Sometimes save humans from drowning, or guide ships to safety. They can be seen sitting on rocks, looking into mirrors, combing their long hair and singing sweetly, luring men to marry them so they can gain a soul. *Mermen*, on the other hand, are ugly, with green hair, and they cause storms and tidal waves, drowning and devouring humans and then stealing their souls. They do not marry mortals and are said to eat their own children. The *Blue Men of Scotland* are *Merpeople* who throw rocks at ships and cause storms at sea but can be defeated by rhymes, which confuse them. Also *Merrymaids*, *Merwives*, *Merwomen*.

MERROW *Moruadh Murrughach Murdhuachas* (IRELAND). Similar to

The Court of Faerie, Edmund Dulac, 1910.

Merpeople – top half human, lower half fish – the males have green hair and teeth, red noses, piggy eyes and short flipper-like arms. The females are beautiful with webbed fingers.

MORGAN LE FAY From *Arthurian legends*, ruler of *Avalon*. Beautiful, powerful water faery, who can shapeshift into any animal or bird. Carried dying *Arthur* to *Avalon* on a ship. Also *Morgan Le Fée*, *Morgaine*, *Morgana*, *Morganette*.

MURYANS (CORNWALL). Meaning '*ant*'. The Cornish believed that faeries were the souls of ancient heathens or druids, who got stuck between Heaven and Hell and shrank to the size of ants, then vanished because each time they shapeshifted they lost power and stature.

NANNY BUTTONCROP *Nanny Buttoncap* (YORKSHIRE). A good nursery faery, who guards children at night, making sure they are warm and safely tucked up in their beds.

NIKKISEN *Nyker* (ISLE OF MAN). Water faeries, who live in *Nikkisen's pool*. They lure humans into the water, then lead the souls of the drowned in procession, under the light of the full moon.

NIMBLE MEN *Fir Clis* (SCOTLAND). *Sky faeries*, associated with *Will O' The Wisp* and the *Northern Lights*, said to be *elves* dancing in the moonlight.

NUCKLELAVEES *Nuckelavees Nuchlavis* (SCOTLAND). *Sea faeries*, ill-tempered, hideous, malevolent to humans. Usually half-man, half-horse, no hair or skin. Having no skin, their red muscles and white sinews are clearly visible, along with their black blood flowing through yellow veins. They cause sickness in livestock and humans, bring drought, hate the rain, and will not cross fresh water.

OAKMEN (ENGLAND). *Tree faeries*, or *forest dwarves* with red noses and red toadstool caps. Guardians of the sacred oak, the forest and all its animal inhabitants. Human intruders who offended them by felling oaks, or hunting animals were offered poisonous fungi enchanted to look like delicious food.

OBERON King of the faeries, connected to Arthurian legend, mentioned by Shakespeare in *A Midsummer Night's Dream*. It is said he may have been *Tronc*, a hideous dwarf, whom the faeries turned into their handsome king. Cursed with short stature by an evil faery at his christening.

OLD MAN WILLOW (ENGLAND). *Willow tree faery*, said to reach out and 'snatch' at passers by, especially in remote, lonely places.

OUPHE (EUROPEAN). Mountain nymph, dim-witted faery, or elf, usually left as changelings. Possible source of the word '*oaf*'. '*Ouph*' was an Elizabethan word for Elf.

PECH (SCOTTISH LOWLANDS). Underground faeries with long arms, red hair and huge feet, which they could turn up over their heads to shelter from the rain. They built many of the ancient Scottish castles and churches, only working at night. Also *Pecht, Peht* and *Pict*.

PHOOKA (IRELAND). Irish *Hobgoblins*, can appear in many forms, either half-human, half-horse, an old man in tattered clothes, or a goat, horse, dog, bull or eagle. Can be helpful to farmers or millers, play tricks on travellers, steal potatoes and babies, haunt the dreams of drunkards and kill cattle. Also *Phouka, pooka* or *Puca*.

PHYNNODDEREE *Fenoderee Fenodyree* (ISLE OF MAN). Hairy Manx house faeries or *Brownies*, incredibly strong, with long arms. Not very clever, but very kind and hardworking, unless offended.

PILLIWIGGINS Tiny little winged faery guardians of the spring flowers, particularly those growing near the oaks where they live. Ride from flower to flower on bees. Their beautiful, blonde seductive *Queen Ariel* wears delicate white clothes, sleeps in a cowslip, controls the winds and rides a bat. She cannot speak, only sing very beautifully.

PIXIES A *Pixie* or *Pixy* is small with pointy ears and nose and arched eyebrows, shiny delicate wings and often dressed in green, wearing a toadstool or foxglove cap. Can't touch iron, hates laziness, loves dancing, music, big parties, mischief and playing pranks, although can be helpful to deserving humans. Also *Pisgies, Pixys, Piskies, Pigseys*. Probably relates to the *Picts* of Scotland.

PLANT RHYS DWFEN (WALES.) Family of *Rhys the deep*. Lovely, honest, kind little faeries, who live in a land made invisible by a magical herb, and ruled by *Rhys Dwfen*. Possibly half-human, very honest, generous, rich and successful at auctions.

POBEL VEAN (CORNWALL). *Small People* or faeries of the South West of England. The females are fair and wear crinolines, fine lace, jewels and pointy hats. Males are dark-skinned, dressed in blue or green, wearing tricorn hats with silver bells. All are youthful with large brown eyes. Said to be the spirits of those who cannot go to heaven; must stay on earth, shrinking until they vanish. Seen only by those who put a four-leaf clover on their head.

PORTUNES (ENGLAND). Oldest of the English faeries. They appear as very small (less than one inch tall), wrinkly old men, wearing coats of patched cloth. Like *Leprechauns*, they are pranksters and guard treasure. If captured, they will grant a wish.

POUQUES (CHANNEL ISLANDS). Similar to the English *Puck*, associated with the devil. Often seen wheeling a barrow full of parsnips. Short, strong, ugly, hairy, long arms, dressed in scruffy clothes. Can be kind and helpful as house faeries, love cream, but are offended and will disappear if given generous gifts. The women spin flax.

PUCK *Poake Pouke* (ENGLAND). Mischievous woodland faery prankster. Described as a jester, can make humans dance when he plays his pipes. Sometimes appears as a horse, tricking humans to ride him. Other times he is . a child, eagle, donkey or a half-human half-goat, playing pipes like Pan. May merrily lead people into bogs then disappear (hence the phrase '*Pouke-led*', '*Pixy-led*', or '*Pouk-ledden*'). Originally a demon, but later

Firmin Bouisset, from Contes du Pays d'Armour, 1890.

associated with *Robin Goodfellow*, *Jack Robinson* and *Robin Hood*.

PWCA *Pwca* (WALES). Related to the English *Puck*. Head like a bird, tadpole-like figure. Can be house faeries, or *Will O' The Wisp*, or pranksters.

PYRENEES (CORNWALL). Dwell invisibly among the standing stones of Cornwall, making them walk, dance or even sing.

RED CAP (SCOTLAND). Known in Ireland as *Fir Larrig*. Nasty, solitary, scrawny, grey-haired, old man, his cap dyed red with fresh human blood. Has leathery skin, long grey hair, buck teeth, skinny arms and long claw-like talons. Wears heavy boot, carries a pikestaff and guards castle ruins and cairns, attacking intruders with a wooden scythe. Will disappear if you hold up a cross, leaving behind only a talon or tooth.

REDSHANKS (SOMERSET). Pipe-smoking faeries, who are said to be the spirits of the Danes who were killed near Dolbury Camp, in Somerset.

ROANE (IRELAND, SCOTLAND). Race of *faery seal people*, from the Islands of Scotland and Ireland. Similar to the *Selkies*, but much more gentle and peaceful.

ROBIN GOODFELLOW (ENGLAND). Male head, body of a goat, also known as *Puck*, *Pan* or *Jack Robinson* (as in 'before you can say…'). Son of a faery father and a mortal mother.

ROBIN HOOD (ENGLAND). Lives in the forest, dresses in green, steals from the rich, helps the poor. Sometimes thought to be based on a real person, usually assumed to be a nature spirit, synonymous with *Robin Goodfellow* and *Puck*.

SALEERANDES (WALES). Scaley Welsh faeries, look like two-legged lizards. Frightening to look at, but never harmful. Cold-blooded, naked and always cold, they seek out the warmth from a human-made fire. Probably related to the *salamander*, the elemental representing fire.

SEA MITHER (ORKNEY). Sea mother, or sea spirit, representing summer and life. Her enemy is *Teran*, the spirit of winter. Their battle begins each spring equinox, until he is defeated, so that she can bring warmth, life and growth to the sea and land around the Isles of Orkney. *Teran* comes back at autumn equinox to fight again, until she is defeated and banished, and has to listen to the cries of drowning fishermen, as he unleashes the cold, dangerous, stormy weather.

SEA TROWS Trows who have been banished by the land Trows to live at the bottom of the sea. Look like deformed monkeys, with strangely sloping heads, flat round feet, webbed fingers and toes and hair like seaweed. They are stupid and mischievous and like to steal and play tricks on fishermen. Rarely come out of the water, as they can only move very slowly on dry land.

SECRET FOLK (ENGLAND). Euphemism for faeries. Also *Secret People*.

SEELIE COURT (SCOTLAND). Blessed troop of faeries who are heard but never seen. They are totally good, heroic and beautiful, riding the wind, searching for good deeds to be done, and acting as judges in disputes between faeries. Opposite to the bad faeries of the *Unseelie Court*.

SELKIES (SCOTLAND, ORKNEY). *Sea faeries*, similar to *merpeople* but appear as seals. They can shed their sealskins and come ashore to dance as beautiful women or handsome men. Some come to live in the mortal world, but usually they lure humans to marry them in their world, though never against their will. Also known as *Silkies*, *Selchi*.

SHELLEY COATS (SCOTLAND). Small mischievous *water-bogles* or faeries, which haunt shallow, freshwater streams, pools and woodland lakes. They have fishy-looking round bodies, covered in red or purple shell-like scales, and large mouths and eyes. They can fly and see well at night. Like to trick or confuse travellers who stop to drink and scare swimmers away.

SHEOGUES (IRELAND). Also known as *Sheogues*, *Shopes*, *Sigh Oges* or Sidheog. Live in *raths* (ancient forts, surrounded by circular mounds) or thorn bushes. Make beautiful enchanted music, which inspires musicians and poets or lures humans into bogs. Usually friendly, but have been known to kidnap children and leave behind a changeling who will only live for a year.

SHOCKS (ENGLAND). Evil shapeshifting faeries or may be ghosts. They appear as a dog or cow with a shaggy mane and eyes like saucers, or a human with a donkey's head and a nasty bite.

SHONEY (ISLE OF LEWIS). A type of *kelpie*, usually male, always ugly stupid and ill-tempered, with sharp teeth and pointy ears. The islanders would brew ale, then offer a cup to the Shoney, in return for abundant fishing and seaweed to fertilise the soil. Also *Shony*, *Spony*.

SIDHE Irish and Scottish Gaelic name for faeries. Usually dressed in white with long hair and care for animals. When offended by a human they can cause illness or worse. They steal pretty girls to be their bridesmaids and kidnap babies, replacing them with changelings. They appreciate offerings of milk, food, tobacco and whiskey. Originally the name 'sidhe' referred to gods, then became used for witches, spirits and anything supernatural. Another name for *burial mound* or *barrow*, where they are said to live. Also *Shee*, *Si*, *Sith*.

SILKIES (NORTH OF ENGLAND). Small usually female house faeries or *brownies*. Dress in white or grey silk and enjoy housework, but if offended or feeling mischievous, may behave like a poltergeist or terrorise lazy servants.

SLEIGH BEGGY (ISLE OF MAN). Believed to be the original inhabitants of the island. Small and naked with feet like a crow. Live underground, on riverbanks or underwater. Steal racehorses. Can prevent them entering your house with silver, ashes, salt and yellow flowers (except broom). Also *Sleih Beggey*, *Yn Sleigh Veggy*, *Mooinjer Veggey*.

SLUAG (SCOTLAND). *Sluagh* Pronounced sloo-a. Evil faeries, 'the host' or the souls of the damned, fly from the west in black clouds, forced to haunt the scenes of their sins forever. To keep them away from a sick room, any west-facing windows must be kept shut. Related to

56

When Everything was ready down came the Trolls, Reginald Knowles, 1910.

the *Unseelie Court*. It is possible they were originally the sky elementals. Sometimes spirits of stormy weather.

SPRIGGANS (CORNWALL). Small, wizened, nocturnal faeries dressed in green with red caps. Said to be ghosts of humans or giants. Can inflate themselves until as big as giants and cause whirlwinds that blight crops. They steal from humans, kidnap babies and replace them with hideous spriggan changelings. They fiercely defend their treasure with arrows, spears and slings but are afraid of salt water.

SPRITES (from the Latin '*spiritus*'). Any spirit, soul or ghost. Also used as generic term for faeries, especially those who are invisible, or seem less earthy and more elusive. Sprites paint the changing colours of autumn leaves.

SPUNKIES (SCOTLAND, ENGLAND). Another name for *Will O' The Wisps*, sometimes believed to be the souls of unchristened children, often seen coming to church to meet the recently dead on *Midsummer Eve*. Similar to the Scottish *Tarans*.

TARANS (SCOTLAND). Like English *Spunkies*, they are unchristened children who cannot go to heaven so wander the earth forever. To meet one is potentially fatal but if you sprinkle them with holy water and speak the baptism rite, you may save its soul.

TIGHE FAERIES (ISLE OF MAN). Relatives of the Scottish *house brownie*, they do household chores at night, taking good care of fireplaces and animals (but will not live with cats). They dislike loud noises and expensive rewards, only accepting food and drink in return for their work.

TOM THUMB A childless couple visited *Merlin*, who predicted the woman would bear a child who would grow no larger than a thumb. The boy grew into a man within four minutes. The Queen of the faeries was his mother's midwife and his faery godmother, and she gave him magic powers. He was eaten by a salmon, then served up at King Arthur's court, where he stayed.

TOOTH FAERIE Leaves a silver coin, found the next morning, in exchange for a child's milk tooth when left under the pillow at night.

TOM TIT TOT (ENGLAND). An alternative name for *Hobgoblin*. Name of a goblin in an English version of *Rumpelstiltskin*.

TROWS *Drows* (SHETLAND). Like the Scandinavian *Troll*. Also known as *Nightcreepers* or *Nightstealers*. There are *Land Trous* or *Sea Trous* (see earlier reference).

TUATHA DÉ DANANN (IRELAND). Early inhabitants of Ireland, originally from Greece. Brought magical powers and artefacts with them. Defeated by the *Milesians* and banished to the faery '*burghs*' (mounds) or under lakes. They shrank in size and became invisible to humans. Enjoy chess and hurling. Credited with constructing stone circles.

TWLWYTH TEG (WALES). Fair-haired faeries dressed in white, who live under the ground or water in an enchanted garden, from which nothing can be taken without disappearing. Their rulers *King Gwydion* and *Queen Gwenhidw* live in the stars, coming out at night, sometimes leaving presents in welcoming houses with warm fires. Said to exchange money for faery coins, which disappear when you try to spend them.

UILEBHEIST (SHETLAND, ORKNEY). Guardians of the sea around the islands, they appear as many headed sea monsters or sea dragons. Also known as *Draygans*.

UNSEELIE COURT (SCOTLAND). Unblessed or uncanny evil faeries, said to be the souls of the damned, sometimes flying, kidnapping and enslaving mortals and making them throw elf bolts at others. They dwell in the underworld beneath Scottish mountains. All malevolent faeries belong to the *Unseelie Court*.

URISKS (SCOTLAND). A wrinkly, scrawny, half-human, half-goat, with duck feathers and patches of hair and is so deformed and ugly it can frighten you to death. They like humans and seek their company, rewarding them with assistance of any kind. They are highly intelligent and intuitive, even psychic and haunt desolate pools.

WAG BY THE WAY (SCOTLAND). Faery guarding the roads for Scottish nobles.

WAG-AT-THE-WA' (SCOTLAND). Sometimes guards the byways of the Lowlands. Ugly, little old man, with crooked legs and long tail, wearing a red coat, blue trousers, grey cloak. He has a nightcap tied round his face, as he suffers from toothache. Disapproves of strong alcoholic drinks.

WATER FAERY Deceptive in their beauty, the females will seduce young men and steal their souls, while the males are bad tempered and malicious. Also *Water Nymph*.

WATER LEAPER *Llamhigyn y dwr* (WALES). Vicious Welsh water faeries, appear like a small toad with bats' wings and tails instead of legs. They drown fishermen and drag sheep under the water to eat them.

WATER-SHEERIE (IRELAND). Alternative name for *Will O' The Wisp*.

WATER WRAITH (SCOTLAND). Scowling, female water spirit, said to appear mostly to people who are drunk.

WAYLAND SMITH (ENGLAND). Reportedly *King of the Elves* who resides at *Wayland Smithy*, a chambered long barrow in Wiltshire. Legend says that if a horse is tethered overnight at Wayland Smithy it will be magically shod by morning.

WEATHER FAIRES Generic term for spirits or elementals of wind, rain, sun, storm etc.

WEE FOLK (SCOTLAND, IRELAND). Faeries.

WEE WILLY WINKIE (SCOTLAND) *Sandman* in Europe. Faery of sleep and pleasant dreams.

WELL SPIRITS *Well Guardians*. Keepers of wells, springs and other water sources.

WHITE DOBBIE (SCOTLAND, ENGLAND). Partnered by a wildly staring white hare with bloodshot eyes, this faery resembles a frail, lifeless human wearing a dirty white coat.

WHITE LADY Interchangeable with '*ghost*' or '*faery*', this apparition is known the world over as a '*genius loci*', or '*spirit of the place*', and is particularly noted as the guardian of wells, springs, rivers and bridges. She is also synonymous with *Guinevere* of Arthurian legend, which in its original form '*Gwenhwyvar*' means 'white phantom'. The Irish white phantom '*Bean Fionn*' means 'white lady'.

WILL O' THE WISP Spectral light that flickers over marshes, bogs and swamps. Said to be the souls of dead children or lost souls trapped between heaven and hell. Some say that witnessing this phenomenon is an omen of ill-fortune, even death. Also *William With The Little Flame* or *Will O' The Wykes*.

WISH HOUNDS *Wist Hounds Wisht Hounds* (DEVON, CORNWALL) A pack of black, headless, ghostly hounds that haunt Wistman's Wood on Dartmoor, hunting human souls. They are also said to hunt the demon Tregeagle in Cornwall, accompanied by their huntsman, the Devil. Also *Yell Hounds* or *Yeth Hounds*.

WITCH Sometimes interchangeable with '*hag*' or '*faery*'. Said to possess magical powers and an intuitive knowledge of herbs and potions. Can conjure magical spells and fly through the air on a broom stick or '*ragwort stalk*'. Often seen seated at a spinning wheel, weaving spells, both good and evil. Able to change their appearance to seduce men and bring them under their spell.

WOMAN OF THE MIST (ENGLAND). Said to appear as an old woman collecting sticks at the side of the road, then to disappear into the mist. A '*hag*' or '*faery*' of Somerset tradition.

WRYNECK (LANCASHIRE, ENGLAND). Evil spirit or faery, said to be even worse than the Devil.

YALLERY BROWN (EAST ANGLIA). Perhaps the most evil of faeries, this '*Yarthkin*' was discovered under a stone, cocooned in his own '*yellowy brown*' hair and beard. If you stop to help Yallery Brown, you will be blighted with misfortune for the rest of your life.

YARTHKIN *Earth-kin* (ENGLAND). East Anglian *Earth Faery* and *Water Faery*. Also *Tiddy Mun*.

The Prince Enters the Wood, Richard Doyle, 1866.